things done for themselves

things done for themselves

preverbs

George Quasha

M
H
P

Marsh Hawk Press
East Rockaway, NY • 2015

Marsh Hawk Press books are published by Poetry Mailing List, Inc., a not-for-profit
corporation under section 501 (c) 3 United States Internal Revenue Code.

Cover art: Axial Drawing from the Dakini Series [#3, 11-16-14, 18"×24", acrylic
paint on paper] by George Quasha from the collection of Herbert C. Lust.
Book design: Susan Quasha

Publication of this book was supported by a generous grant from the Community of
Literary Magazines and Presses via the New York State Council on the Arts.

Library of Congress Cataloging-in-Publication Data

Quasha, George.
  [Poems. Selections]
  Things done for themselves : preverbs / George Quasha. — First edition.
     pages cm
  ISBN 978-0-9906669-5-0 (pbk.) — ISBN 0-9906669-5-6 (pbk.)
  I. Title.
  PS3567.U28A6 2015b
  811'.54—dc23
                              2015023921

16 17 18 19 20   5 4 3 2 1   First Edition

Marsh Hawk Press
P.O. Box 206
East Rockaway, NY 11518-0206
www.marshhawkpress.org

from the beginning preverbs are
for Susan Quasha

preverbs

pre focus

For the Eye altering alters all

WILLIAM BLAKE

If I close my eyes to imagine a book, no book appears. In my world books don't come to be by prefiguring them. They are nothing if not self-generating concrete acts taking their place among *things, entities*. And yet they may rival those they move among, even alter the status of the ordinary real things we thought we knew. And for every doubt raised about the known world a further doubt rebounds upon the book that set it going. If the book alters my sense of the real, the altered real reconfigures the book. Reading is the site of this oscillation between things created and things found; in one moment they reflect each other and in the next they switch places. Reader, now indistinguishable from writer, is caught in the middle. As in life? *And* as in the dark. I recall that after several days in true darkness and not a ray of light there were moments when I no longer knew if my eyes were open or closed, or indeed if I was awake or asleep. I came to imagine a special sense of mimesis, perhaps with a post-Wildean twist: in the middle of the work—which means at any point inside—neither art nor life knows what came first, nor, perhaps, where either begins or ends. Art is inventing itself in step with life inventing itself. Or so the mind is saying, here in the dark where it sees by what might be called *lingual light*.

Pre is the state in which *preverb* lives. Its before is where the verb has its play and out of which the book emerges, configuring as it goes. It has no lasting image of itself, yet it's never without self-imaging, so long as something exists, a book, a site. It's a thing done for itself.

How to know it's a line, a poem, a book? Not by rules, nor any other prefiguration. The *bounding line*, to use Blake's term—the self-defining integrity marking the immediate limits of what is happening—is shifting, if not leaping, in bounds. What would an agitating self-organizing *inbound* be but a book, or what occurs in it? It comes to be by self-tracking in sync with the event under hand, which leaves only quasi-interpretable tracks in its wake.

Where the original is always yet to come,
writing and reading do each other's work.

ONTONONYMOUS THE PARTICULAR

This book belongs to a family of books—but *family* lacks the verbal force of terms of venery, say, a *murder of crows*, reflecting perhaps large black birds dining on the dead, an ominous presence. A *blood* of books? a *mind*? a *tongue*....

Back to basics, some things are said about proverbs, their books, their origin and way of thinking about themselves, in a short piece at the end called *pre*.

MARCH 2015, BARRYTOWN, NEW YORK

Book I

things done for themselves

things done for themselves

for Susan

We walk together like a field of fireflies.
It gives the ear back to itself.
Hard to beat being heard.
No word for this thing between us, feeling afield.

Mark the opening eye.
The words I leave out rip me apart.
Your mystery projects the core violating itself, blurted the absent voice.
Dark seeming when I can't seem enough.

Time's recovering, I'm here to quit the garden for good.

Reading poetry suffers it to speak.
Violation is not what you think, unless it is.

Things done for themselves are the only things done for all.

Just walking by she multiplies in futures [*flash*].
I'm the one in the middle longing to be the many.
Put *eye* inside the empty letter and she looks back at you.
Voyeurism's the illusion I'm not looking at myself.
Seeming without seeing.

Exhaust the wisdom impulse before it exhausts paradise.

Today's the day I rewrite my biography.
Pen slips on the slopes of sorrow.
I can't help believing in one thing after another.
Sounds good to me sounds true enough.
And then. And then.

A blurt's a site of first breath.
This only sounds *this* way.
We wave through each other to approach.
And flex and flex.

Optimal includes bottom.

The world's singing to itself again through our dog.
The tremor in the voice lets the knower out.
Poetry is the state stating.
Say what keeps saying what it is.

You didn't know it but it let you know it.
A form is what knows to take place before you.
It gives the eye back to itself.
Seeing marks.

Let's meet in the dark where you read through yourself.
Juliet, the verbal scent.

Names get new life to be spoken.
And so *I* makes my ascent into present.
Poetry says it better than it sounds.
If I don't mean what I say at least it means me back.

The only things done for all are the ones done once for themselves.

I barely feel myself hanging together.
She knows to call me by my calling.
It takes a life to be known.
To tone.
Like things fall free alike.

The underline rhythmic is over and out. Over and out.

Hearing marks.
Speak in the first person on earth.

She sets my system on merge.
Meanwhile I call from a verge, *Don't strand me on the grounds of sound.*
I can say nothing I can't hear.

The vision's the body seeing through itself.
The poem even now is hearing itself.

Frog pond in the dark's bounding across from here.

right sounds

Everything sounds true to itself.

Dreaming my language disappearing I asked, "What do you want from me?"
A rite is hearing if accompanied by a hissing sound.

Poem-like dreams fan-dance before inquiring mind.
I hear music with no outside.

The sound of passage is half from the participant, half from the orbit.
I notice when speaking the unspeakable she parts her lips like an ear.

So I'm listening for you. Thank goddess.
Speaking bodies, *you hear!*

We are the shapes we speak.
The world is alive with feedback measured in ears full.

A spherical sound surrounds its own.
The text does the hearing.

Right-sounding lines have more punch per syllable like the weather.
Tearing the heart away is audibly non-separate at this site.

This is where identity finds its way out.
Through the door, according to Confucius. Wisdom billows before me.

The sound of one face slapping is two lips lapping.
Bad jokes rescue the good standing beyond assessment.

The rite impediment making sense violates the right.
I feel feralized.

Mind when a poem is keeping out of jail.
Celebration. This is the leading part. Her curtain's going up.

Getting back to the raw stages.
Don't know where to turn until it turns.

And I still don't know my lines.
Wise sayings never sound right in the wild.

Verily though the shadow walks through me...

What planet is this really, don't you wonder?
Shadow stalks here like rhetorics.

I exert control over the process at hand less and less and....
Less thumb. Less wrist. Less shoulder. Breathe through spine, audibly.

Where the rite happens all clears like being fallen off through.
In caverns I imagine I come ear to ear with my own strangeness.

Everything sounds true to itself. Unless it doesn't.
The missed note hisses still in the blank.

On certain days in certain hours truths are known by tone alone.
Learn a new language every time you open your mouth.

I can't not tell you: the hand is carried by the pen.
Mouth listens till the tongue moves.

Is strangeness the default state of a secret sense?
Eyes glisten till the thought sees.

Think, think, lest the name tame before the tale can tell.
No window, no willow, no wind wallowing in its own moan.

Seeking title I came upon: *The courtless court way of love and affliction.*
Now I'm breathing hard in the sense of place self-seeking.

Things have to come home to themselves.
It speaks to know itself in the return.

friends forever

for Sherry Williams

Imagine yourself for once in step with yourself.
Words catch—scent of passing through my mind before.

Relinquish continuity like facing death a moment at a time.
A thing may feel its groove to be a word in place.

Distinct feeling of a line here before now lost.
The bardo of dying is continuous unto itself, and beyond.

A true line is instant homage to anyone you can read.
Any false, farewell to the same.

Wake up the famous *now*; later try *there*, now infamous.
Friendship teaches: it's a terrible wait to get here.

A thought's a world still looking for an ally.
The things I say to myself are beyond mention.

You know you've had enough when you're sure you aren't dead.
Great lines ultimately strangle on themselves.

These words have strayed from her mind.
All there all the time, as I long to be. *Slow now.*

Tasted truly a thing has tone, smacks of itself, audibly just.
Intimate words press lips open and strike.

Never tear the tone from its tongue in the name of telling tales.
Lips leap here out of single sense.

Identity is already secret.
Trusting time in time tames self itself.

Writing releases its grip to grasp its own distraction.
I retract everything until saying feels like itself.

A true line lifts out of greatness coming up for air at last.
It runs to you as a cherished belief lost in your arms.

Ah, the moral edge, carving one's pain into the being of others.
Poetic words taste of their origin, the devil's wine.

The reader reserves approval until the poem warms up to him. Her.
He checks out the thought like a dog sniffing his old bed. Hers.

Surrender is its own presence—am I here yet?
I track the thought like a god smelling an old altar.

I'm heavy and I wanna be light.
I must have stolen that line from you, how it lifts.

Coda

Parting your lips poetic desire sucks the words right out.
Even now the poem comes thinking it's already you.

turning mind out

I showed up feeling I was not the one expected to be seen.
Welcome to my poem. Lock the door.

I'm here with you expecting only to be new, I found myself saying.
There's a presumption in passing of our being some *where.*
In this sense of the book of changes she wears me. Lines, numbers, forces.
Knowing the world wants knowing.

I'm expecting. The surface is feeling itself.
You'd have to want to be someone else to feel at home.
No known music is being heard—my ears tell me.

Coming here I found again my pulse into the wild.
Bewildering seems to be *finding—self self self self*—sounding secrets.
I say the password unacceptable.

The turning thought honing awareness won't fill this space.
Time retools and I'm in school.
Every moment is never before.

Strange to meet you here in such an intimate place.
Clearly wanting is what being around does to join us.
It's only a line—no, horizon—mountains and valleys rise to its view.

Aware in my center I lay eyes where sky meets earth.
I'm going out to enter my cave in the world so to speak.

Waking between.

Poem matrix is going outside now.
World skin is feeling itself inside here.

What's the *matter* is I'm not taking sides, to be literal.

Word tribes sense more purely.
I find myself atremble in their tangle.

Take up residence, fling the garden gate open to its stone tone.
If the music evades I turn the attention.

Dancing defies the gravity of the situation.
Still listening is the point of between.

Like attracts the traction to track her. *Faster! Faster!*

The logic of the way through is lodged as the legs go.
Toodle-loo or *shoo* show the sheer path, split in two.
À *tout à l'heure* or *boo*, a third way's all in one breast.
Rime time and beyond, of which fond wishes betray us.
There's a music of the gears I still hear, so much time ago. Show time.

There the dance is the sense of the six: face back around to see outfront.
Lines are everywhere I forget the count.
Unwobble the way, Confucius say.

Along this surface I don't dare expect, for fear of invoking intolerably more.
Never get all you wish. Hear me out. She also say.

Every moment looks at itself in your mirror.
Turn around quick, life is slipping away unnoticed.

The all-in-one breast is never at rest.
That's the kind of book that finds.

Telltale yarrows are flying… Let the line flap.
Stock up on heart-deafening slogans is the disorder of the day.

Invite your worst to join you here—no party, just jointure, the subliminal alight.
Writing edges the view—lets look as look reads.

Dowse for your spot, said the old line to the newcomer.
She undresses to address—I watch slowly to receive.

Sometimes it wishes in me that I be the poet.
But then it closes me back down around, the better to open out.

Gesture exposure's the sun setting in her apparel.
Flesh tones to the looker, songwear for embodied silence.

Jump in, get your mind wet, time's got you surrounded.
The bounding line inbounds your given acts possible to conceive.

The status of the present thought is not the thought before it.
Reading births boundingly.

This meditation on meditation as reading is not premeditated.
It follows the third degree, as if to wish a way away.

Lift your burden along the line of full reckoning—until it beckons release.
Just because I'm reading I'm not exempt, but I can pretend.

Earth calls for more ear-rending shibboleths to wrench her song free.
Hold on, getting warmer, wait, perhaps we can almost meet.

They say time will tell—or is it still holding back?
Reading on a sliding scale—ride or slip, the advantage is relative.

That's me on the left, you, right, and paginal space holds us between.
Look, the wall, a dagger—tent stake?—At last, the big light show!

Read on, the walrus said, one two, and through.
Nowhere fast. *Nothing* lasts fast.

What time holds back is intolerable to the knower.
Pressing on makes tracks in the timeline.

At any given point it makes you think you want to know more.
If you weren't listening now this line would still be emptying.

But here comes the sheriff. The pressure is mounting.
Quiet down, axial force is gathering itself between.

If you say so, she says, I say so.
Obedience inquires as inquiry obeys.

That's her dancing in the window with her curtain going up.
The line is a hearing aid but you can still come closer.

The whites of their eyes are never really white.
It's no wonder we know next to no one.

Don't lose that thought by getting lost in it.
Precise listening creates silence necessarily.

Take me to your mother, I want to thank her for my pleasure.
No hope is happy being hope. Give it a hand.

Don't look back to hear on track—the choo-choo may be coming.
Here's the kicker on the gods glancing—it's your eyes they catch.

A line is reaching toward its mirror.
Reflection is already further.

Sound alarms so angels sense.
This is the language of a majority of one.

To say we is to be abreast.
So it says in the commentary: Cloud eggs scramble ideas in an otherwise clear sky.

Just because you think it doesn't make it yours.
Nothing is more poetic than driving meaning out of town.

The poet is an ant dutifully carrying nutriment to the core: lore.
The rhythm of trudge rehabilitates time.

Prophetic tells outside.
Like tongues like bodies. Birds!

Keep alert, a life might be waving goodbye.
A line of thought thinks its link whence it comes.

Thought territorializes the thought about. Words!
To trace the song's outline shave the note on the other edge.

Mysteries find their way into [*wurdan*]† of their own accord.
Split-second god-glanced eyes your eyes catch lit to the heart of the matter.

Full-frame emptiness.
Pulsation is previous to time.

Language is before saying.
Never disturb what isn't here yet.

---

† Asterisk indicates the Indo-European root, a language reality defined as a word known to be unknown to have existed. Or known to not have existed, as far as we know. The root word for word [*wurdan] reminds us that you have to have a word for the word you can never find.

Weather pleasures before you know it, biblically.
Sounds like angels as tongues sound like bodies.

Two alien thoughts rub against each other—text!
Likewise weather pleasures itself.

Ceaseless weave, Penelope's Klein Bottle loom, lose the thread further, further…
Gut thinking is the performance of itself.

Give the girl her body back.
Poetry is before-saying.

Insistent prosody breeds dysprosody.
Speech reorder, how tongue unties.

How do you get in here between the filaments?
Spread the flaps to let the shaded longing lapse.

The accurately space-prohibitive edges out sludge.
Presumed disorder darkens the science.

Now I'm the guy I used to see in the window seeming to know a thing or two.
Scribble away to scratch the itch of the book.

Variebilitas, said Dante, speaking his language for the language to come.

I know she has a powerful mind when I feel her in my head.
Who you say?

Silly questions protect the under inner side.
Thank you for not letting me explain but…

Beauty educates the relaxation response as the atmosphere thins.
Between a category error and a non-fit is a non-place.

Come out here where the understanding is good. She bares.
You feel fed through.

MA. Outlore.
Impossibility does not bound.

My elective affinity allows me to be a fool rushing in. Startle!
Impossibility limits without limit.

God fell in his image as man.
The unsaid goes before, there to follow.

Now rise up as woman. I dream, I dream.
These words flicker from the out set. I blink.

Outbound eyes. The glance that empties its object.
Erotic study is reciprocal with the studied.

May every word, every phrase, every utterance find its caesura.
I'm here to mount my phoria even as Dante beholds Beatrice in the Star Cart.

Hello, hello, if there's a goddess of language I ask: what is it you want from me?
Exclamation points all around.

The strangeness of impossible naming is inescapable.
Drop back down through a hole in the middle—euphoric euphonics.

Readback bounds me further, down, stretched out and waiting for my eagle.
I come to serve within the swerve.

Now pluck out this belief stuck in my liver, my *live her*, he said.
I'm shaking out the bushes to find the disappearing peacock.

I'm breathing further by the flower.
In the choice between sweet and sour I choose between.

I'm holding a book without end but works back to the beginning.
Eyes light in delight only to relight.

Hail to the book with the hook of thorough, I turn pages between thoughts.
Category errs everywhere of within.

I'm staking out the rushes to bind a misdispersing tree flock.
Thinking thins to let space *in*.

More light, said Goethe, legendary.
That poetry enlightens is apocryphal.

Being on the spot stretches from hell to heaven, roundtrip.
Dread. Having to sing when you can't.

Amapola, trench terror of the song world, with poppies for lips.
Some words heat of their own accord.

Apocryphonics: sounds in hiding from unauthorized authors.
A self-true word twists a little to tell its tale of survival.

Look up spinally.
The way beyond is vertical.

Dying between lets the axis pulse out.
O mirror down the line, *more apocrypha!*

Crack open your rite to let precedent escape in an unknown body.
Bliss hangs out over the abyss, timed out by rime.

Immortality is not waiting to come alive in the face of death.
In the moment, in the thought, in the stone, core, bone, never alone.

Pose as you are. No one will see you.
The idea is what carries from sound into silence.

Sex finds its way in the punctuation.
Or what ecstasy's there for the other, feeding on one's rippled production?

Agency is an unending mystery in action: whoundunit.
Know life inside like the glass filling up.

A line traces as memory's peeling away.
What's the order? *Here.* How do you know? *It shows.*

Of course no self-true thing is ever before any other self-true thing.
Man in his image fell God.

Not every slogan is a sepulcher for the heart of language.
Moral: Don't study the words until they study you.

Ends meet. Sweet, or not.
The impulse it turns out is the moment before.

Words on the move hear their own heat.
Where's your sense of propriety? provokes a fit.

Burden of the line, to bear what must be said.
Maybe, she backtalks, *but a good line gets the girl without you.*

Will the poem return the heart to its upright position?
I should try this thought out in another room.

A roll of the bones will not abolish how we meet.
Longtime, how it feels, disappearing at length, and still turning out.

The view! The view!

what it sounds like to be here

Between us, only you know this is secret.
Beyond this, it's extraordinarily ordinary.

We begin in the middle, which is wherever the edge is a step away.
Wisdom requires that we write our epitaph in every phrase.

I identify with my projection until it turns on me.
One holds back from the two what is equal to itself.

We two, plus me is three. Now we are drawn toward four and counting.
Identity is the play of sames. Like sounds.

Secrets held beyond their time take back your child's spell.
I can't yet tell you what I haven't found in tongue.

Permission ranted, in my dream last night.
I could see through what I say—so I said *hear me, seeing.*

I hear you is the music each thing longs for down to the lowest body rumble.
Poetry? What happens in the poem mind … I feel it in my hands here.

A line free of everything I know is beautiful is beautiful.

I came this way to give myself the slip.
Somewhere along the line a space falls open in the saying.

Suddenly language is flinging open its door inside its outside.
Word birth earth thirst — it figures itself out from binding, bounding.

It's numerous when the eyes are closed.
Time sculpts in view of itself.

You have to go outside to get supplies, your mirror, the other eyes.
I have to cross the line to get you in. Back.

Say when you feel the thought hit.
The art is in getting out of the way.

It's the delay that matters, substantially speaking.
I am still paying *homage to what I hear is so*.

Number sounds the way it feels. All these years.
I sense myself cut off, yet still rounding on the edges.

The surface means through contact, the way the word surfs.
The hunt is on for unquotable lines.

Dinner is served.

If you turn your mind quick it startles to further life.
Everything tells us its tale on time.

A thinking object shines in the dark.
The book opens itself in… consort!

I long for the words she licks into being.

What weighs in a voice gives it rise.
I am not the thing said where I am most me.

The truth is written all over your face. She's back at it.
I say things I don't know, still in their throat.
Believe nothing you're told, even if true.

Lend me your fears.

Poem learns itself real once able to cry out in its silence.
Gospel is reading itself to wake.

I'm riding on empty.
Life is passing me by.
Sea breezes. I wave.
No hands.

Still mind is moving.
The occasion itself is turning.

You're history, she said. I know, I said.

Like sounds like each other in your ears.
Let the mind show true, clear through, blue.

This space has not yet played its hand, and I'm still without.

Here is where you never know how.
Every order heard speaks *secret* to itself.

Hold in the clear this self-parsing's particular patina.
Listening grips at a glance.

I find myself building what is taking itself apart.

Stay where you are, you're on the following page.
History is not on the other side of the unlimited, although it's turning.

You can't take here from there.
Never is longer than necessary.

Silence is deeper when the voice sounds true.

There is no same page to say on.
Ever is longer than never. Just this once.

Extending my hand bounds over this far to you.
Any life holds a book of it all to be written.

Feeding is always already *back*.
Nothing is final. Feel the gap reach right down into you.

I'll change my mind tomorrow, for now is unchanging.
Long in the line for the poem of no impermeable outside.
Klein poetics: one surface suffices to get past the end in the beginning.

A mantra bound to breakthrough: this is just for me.
This is not all I mean. Time surfaces.

Long in the tooth, haul in the line.
The agent is changing hands faster than before your eyes.

Heavy carrying at length in lode lane.
Skipping the stone unburdens the way magnetic.

Still tracking meaning looking up under word, whoosh, hand over head.
Attraction tracts, seeing stars, earth holds tight.

Never enough, always too much.
Such soundness.

You can only say what hears in you.
Feel what has its way with you, in you.

A word shifts shape to cross the page.
Follow what follows.

There is no same word.
We are only hearing in hollows.

Time feels in me with its waking wedge, and I spring open to awful things.

Every new line a cast out, out of the known. Blown out.

Brain, tattler.

Rain, blessing break, wash out, getting through.

Rattler. How it is hereabouts. And outer. Sounding out of it.

A thousand roots of feeling tamper the ground for this abundance.

A thought is a turning point where beauty is fall out.
Words may whisper together in a faint and private language.

It peaks for itself.
You too uproot knowing all the way here.

Lines too busy looking ahead fail in their tracks to hear each other.
Mind has to stretch all the way out to get the bounce back.

Wise words avoid you.

She dreamt she saw the root of ignorance and it was a root. *Rampant.*
If you don't know mind you won't mind.

A pointing turn thinks itself.
Self-true thought wanders a long low way in mind *quick.*

If the turning head draws the horizon this is my headline.
The poetic teaches my knots to slip.

Anything said truly says further.

Feeling *grasshopper* shows the tall grass *roots up*.
Close your eyes seeing eyes seeing.

Reality startles in response to you as none other.

Spit it out like a true proverb—well then it contradicts itself—tearfully.
Words feel better when they get back out of a poem.

Once heard.
One word twice leaves its same behind.

Knowing what it takes to be here now it takes itself back.
Between any two words is a story in hiding.

What then is natural? always wants answering.
The fit is there before you.

Anything predicts its own more.
Mind draws on what it draws.

Dreaming it that the frame bite back to feed.
I am tracking tales with no trails on this side of sense.

Heaven is just over there.
Speaking the other truth to the other side of you.

The site attracts the meaning.
Zero in here—*I'm thinking of you.*

Nothing repeats forever. Nor even once.
I uproot to know you all the way over.

The wait is not the want.
No time, like the present.

poetic faith

I'm behind in my delight, I said in the dream, out of step with myself.
Reminded again, say what wants saying or *go pure product crazy!*
The chariot is arriving. Found poetry here.

My country tears of thee.
World at five's still hearing pure.

Facts act on my behalf and there's another half, a her in here.
For the time being mind spreads, legs stride, I go wider.
The reflexive poetic drives toward further inflection.

Alternatively *die miserably for want of* finding.
The Orphic mirrors over the edge only just reflecting further.

Ever on the crooking trail of how it means to mean.
She comes up behind with her flowering spine.
As if I know who, she says I do.

I follow the listening.

I'm reaching toward the root through throat, the grunt preceding the world.

Torque tracks a new twist at the heart of your tone.
Incursion inbounds.
Falling into place is not a matter of attitude pitter-patter.

Skintone pattern racket.
Cell's intellect, sounds as old as the hills.
Writing *beyond*, till telling all will wail *ursprung!*

Impermanence is as impermanence does, *no doubt*, nothing stays clear.
Or from the empty heart radiant, still cry, *I'm so foolish a song is heat.*
Is zero knowing wherefore one into zero won't go? No show.

Flow bounds.
Law of the preverse: Every time she says it true *wake up!*
Ur-rime potentiates inverse sonorous reclaiming.

Strange work world where no one knows what you're doing.
Living at cross purposes yourself included and long dark corridors showing.

3

3   *line tongues deeper to surface*

Clamorous remains trace.
If what I say kills what is said is not presence served?
Seduction perverses in the sense of balance.

Trust or bust. Swerve or bow down to the imp of reverse.
The poem studies itself abolishing the repetitive lure.
Yet to return. Take your time in touchback.

Burn, speaking in the surface tense.
Meet me at the grave site of possible delight, *mon frère!*
Disturb my sleep, let me cry.

The restless *I* sees even itself with peripheral incision.
The tongue turns on the self sounding out.
The bleeding edge meets the reading ledge.

Messages in a Klein bottle set out on resurfacing sea.
A language *direct*—from behind—the seeing luxuriant blind.

Sediment of regimen dredges in sound decay.
Sit it away : dance the day down.
Thinking is sinking in place.

Gazing from the blank to take hold through the gown, I let her disappear further.
Caressing the wit a line reads back until it falls off.
Holy is dislodging my sentence as I serve time.

Never again declares *new, now. Want of the letter.*
I believe believing takes leave of itself before living mind.
Meditate moderates *medicate*, speaking modestly for a change.

Forgive this tripartite tree of giveaway habit.
I repent to turn it all around aground.
And if I pray it calls out the power to sustain see-through.

The rough words give over to fluid angles fleshing out.
Still time—still poem—the wish as long as being here.

words live beyond their saying

for Robert Kelly

We are at the center of the world so long as you are reading.
Shadowing blue through silk she shows her sheer view.

Anything breaks out when seen through.
I was an object until your eyes found me.

I think with her world.
She thanks for me.

I am an exhibition.
Everyone here is incognito. So I know you.

Any line reads a stretch of life, as I live in reaching for her.
A fast one leaves thought behind in a trail of feeling dust.

More is the promise I'm made for.
We hit zero to rise again with sweet nothing in the heart.

World surfaces mind.
Every saying reaches toward its bone.

Anything done to another takes everything away.
Letting the cat out of the bag changes nothing, as you know.

Fuse me in your hearing aware — I ask that you taught me.
This slippery act of penciling nothing traces as we speak.

Art's my dare to go barely on the line. Now's getting ready.
The old world still thinks itself in your every cell-bound swivel.

If a poem throws itself at your feet, let it feel you dancing over it.
It's a ride in hiding. Don't tell a soul.

A moment awake embraces through itself.
The excitement dies or flies with equal candor.

I am growing in confidence that it sings itself without me.
Feel this vanishing passion float free right here.

Re*fuse* me who comes to pieces altogether.
Staged torsion is a swindle on a spindle.

Brain evolves in seeing itself, so it is thought.
I talk funny to lift a tongue ban—this tune dances to you too.

Forgive my rushing, it's all down line to catch an influx.
Smile when you reach for your thought, *salud!*

Bang sounds in mind as well, and *bhaga*—like life shaking like life.
Softer seems loftier but wearyingly hard of listening.

Mind claims its right to devolve within hearing.
Some things go over the line only to get further in.

Sounds like you heard it all before—like life feeling twice.
Doing your work *before* you know who you've always been.

Flap a line to hear its spiritual extension.
The shadow knows the sheer view precedes nothing, least of all itself.

A given line inlines many lines.
Someone's breathing heavy spacing out the site.

A verbal object grows in suspense some dense where along the line.
Spissitudo! Spit out a spirited word thing thick with reach.

It's immaterial to me and big all over.
Only mind turning asks *Who is this stone?* and gets a response.

In its fire a voice separates from its allure.
A sail line blown by winds bounds life against death.

Ask permission for everything.
Poems break loose for those from the other side.

Nota bene the terrestrial forms in bounding lines.
Loved the body and it wasn't really there—that's dance for you.

Matter rouses.
Nothing is safe here.

Shocking the track shakes a clinging object free.
A line maps a tongue's tie onto its thought.

Willing to inform she makes asking possible.
Being told you can teach makes it true.

How else does the field say past knowing and know it?
Reversing her breathing startles air into aether.

Lips along this headline may speak us to ourselves.
Thank you for breathing me further.

A field so big only a lifting gesture means inside.
Sheer missing matter restores in the feel of it.

Tension releases in holding tenses.
The sharp edge keeps softness aloft.

Here to find the panic point where inwardly I disappear.
Deployed at last in undersense, undercover's unlearned tense.

I feel myself differently—etheric caesura—doubly bounding.
Still hearing her hearing cuts the point free, still.

On one foot my other comes down in its time.
In these hands I am most like me.

BOOK II

witnessing the place awake

mouth surfing

for Barbara Leon

Speaking with chilies in your mouth produces gustatory sweating.
Think wild of stones.

The poem finds itself resisting reading.
Heat back. Return to the sensible center's facing the flame.

If there's one sure thing it's imbalance in denial.
Reading suffers the ledge to tone down silence.

Suck on her braid to abrade the tongue.
She teaches me to sit in landslide glory.

Lift your lips off the words and they run straight to me, she said.
Maxims magnify *unsayable* into *optimal minimal*.

And if the long-sought free point can't access *beyond*?
The hand writing races the line to end before bending back.

Surfing surfaces like licking lips backtrack to tell their tale.
There's no reading the same line twice.

Turning tables torque like facing faces.
Relax, there's not much danger of a counterfeit free point.

Swallowing between words may yet sweat out the endorphins.
Delphine hormones predict the titillated tissue.

Look, the edgy boulder is contemplating its swivel.
And rolling stones release their tones.

The same line differs from itself to protect you from your mind.
Pray for spontaneous opinion combustion.

Her focusing mouth speaks hereunder steaming up the gaze.
Dolphins, words, the hot thought hearing the clearing cracks.

a sense of itself

self-skinned vision

A line sets out coming at itself from behind.
How do you know where you stand till the thought meets itself in you?

Enter message, enter tale, and the swirl foretold: *it's telling*.
However many times you say it it makes itself all over.

Are we up to the legible edge?
Questions turn on themselves until furthered.

I am, therefore I ask.
Let the book keep reading awake.

I set out knowing less.
Meaning is *for* before *of*.

Following might discriminate against sudden truth.
Knowing mind touches.

I am music to myself, abandoned in listening.
What part of the body is in playback mode now? Guide me over and in.

The habitual things didn't happen—I wasn't there.
Right reading renders a rainbow double.

Resonance tenses a sense of ending itself from the beginning.
Poetry contains everything you ever wanted to say while saying nothing.

Itself *itself*—hear the anxious longing for the evanescent core?
Estranging pleasure follows realigning.

Poetry is discourse which contended disappears all around itself.
Lines arrange in tense release — bodying time into rainbow.

But I fear getting ahead of myself, seeing an angel that goes before.
Reading knows its ending as a dark it allows.

From the beginning a sense of ending itself tenses resonance.
Repetition confuses.

Tell a friend as if a child.
Orphan poetics, dolphin noetics.

At the heart of reading your own writing proves itself not yours.
What you recall I can't know but you tell *me* like a story.

What's cooking? What's thinking?
I'm sensing a singular periodicity out here on the plane of distinction.

I hold this horizon in place to travel along.
What is pulsing now toward the word for it is not a question.

I blink according to a mysterious criticality.
She offers food for me to think, source unknown.

Rime is time in confusion.
What's said again returns to unsaid.

Hair standing up on your body dancing knows what it's doing.
Ending up knowing less begins here.

Can't take back what takes itself back before you.
I study dolphins for the seamless weave between oblivions.

Behold the crystalline flow holding fast in peaking here.
Seek refuge behind a seed to heed a mind beside you.

Thought rubberbands to mouth a telling child.
Taking in his koan gave a useless feeling of being understood, thankfully.

Please take charge of these words as I fall asleep.
Asking permission to be is backwards.

As the blackbird walks sideways on the branch to eat one thing, I think it over.
I fall into the life of a home of my own, and the fruit knows first in the garden.

Loving the planet is the best reason I know to keep coming here.
Likewise the poetic as vision of itself is no tautology as just now it's showing up.

The mystery's knowing how to be where we are and not.
What time is it? What thought is it?

I have come to study the poem in its nature.
There's no place like stone.

Life feels itself in these strange ways.
Note how its medium at hand predicts the present.

Time is slipping out from under, marked.
Art knows how to be where it is when you don't.

Dying is how his mind comes to sit inside my mind and never really leaves.
So poetry is unsustainable discourse, regenerate in its failures to speak.

I am, therefore I wonder on.
Logos in hiding, logic of silence that there isn't.

I'm still calling names.
The word means what is willing to be said.

Surprise beginning: showing up here moving out, over.
Looking on a living thing continuously never sees the same.

Anything known is unknown again in its saying.
To see you through I draw the circumference to the core.

In my dream a poetry liberates its scholar.
A thing comes to an end when the mind shakes loose.

The poem is now.
There is no end to new.

The word is parting its aperture as we speak.
No search, no perch, just wonder and thunder.

Everything is in transmission, secrets surfacing over all.
New is always here waiting in the cracks.

Lingua poesis meaning itself is on the move out back.
Thrown in these arms wide open here, it stays on, in the whereafter.

Now or not at all.
Called out in the middle of speaking.

True connection is by nature—wild.
Which me? How many ages speak out of a face?

Memory bodies, and this is its surge.
Poetry is surgical, we read the remains.

Wild bug waiting on the leaf edge, until the wind shifts, to ride.
Thinking is not trying to stay.

hearing light walking down

for park lovers

I still feel a trace of the dream passing through.
Lean over this way to find the feel of it.
Sensitive things heard near retain the sense of far.

Walking in the park happens as talk sparks, like taking to her likes.
I see this listening *down* now in a slide to the bottom of the line.
Don't take my word for it unless the sun breaks through, she says.

Turning in gets out — she shouts, *I'm heavy and I wanna be light!*
Some things can only be said with the other mouth.
The colder the medium the hotter she speaks.

Listening inside a squeal's more music than a wheel can bear.
Story unfolding snares to hold you in time.
Wake up, break off.
Work down to the grain of the self-seeding voice.

The music flushes to start fresh.
It's the trees, minding the wind.

One tries again and again to say the one thing that's never the same.

This is a mouth thing.
Two lips count double to bedevil a soft slide into deliverance.

Eyes slave after her in the indefinitional night, so slippery the entry, opener.
Wind as I hear talking blows over the mind.
I am roots, I am branches, no preferences in the deep.

I'm rolled over by your listening, in her turn of phrase.
Ein jede Engel, any one hurt, *ist schrechlich,* is its own angel.

Art touch—finger poking eye—says *Open anyway.*
Who cares if I feel violated by a given reading?

It's happening in any film, any trace, receiving nature.
On how many planes are you sensing *at once?*

A writerly or readerly hand moves to your knee—same difference.
The park collects dreams to site a double spark.

In the middle of her scream I heard prick point laughter musicalize everything.

You'll never believe what I tell you until the last word is written.
Nathalie Sarraute died today saying *words live.*

Feedback from the last cry: *believe on me not.*
Imagining her voice here settles the hurt, releasing music from the stone.
You'll never forgive me for breaking the flow.

Everywhere I can't stop building my house.
Use. Lose. Use. Loose.
Backup to build by ear.
There's no telling where you're from last.
A first thing is a history lost.
This is how we have come upon this place. Found sense.

My park now.
No choice but to speak in live words.

We come to a crossroads—now watch the devil dance.
All for the love of the poem—raise hands. Like flowers.

Mudra of Madam Edwarda—gracing my palm today in Paris. It joy'd!
Three dashes to the realm of desire—and fourth the axis in a love cross.

Blessings. Bruisings. Wound tight in heart.

Site incursion specifies life.
Stony angelics implant these mental relics.

Transrelational frolics, O happy subversion.
Taste the air that breathes speaking.

This wildly excursive free point messages.
Never to know in advance how you're feeling.

Build by ear, raze by eye, live what you hear, pray in that you lie.

The crux: Did you write this or did I?
I ask you eye to eye.

Sometimes I sit, mostly I stand.
Even when sitting I'm standing—all the way down.

Hidden *she* sucks seed to seize the sea's deed.
You heard it happen before it did. Music.
It's not poetic but does your noetic. Muse.

What comes accords. Breaks in through.
There's no comparison. It's just between.
I call incursion what gets in through the back door mind.

Did Blake break the news in two to re*fuse*?
What stands between confuses us.
It takes time to know what is being said, *called* lifetime.

To make a space let it fill.
Speech comes up from its own well.
Things tell all as only they fall.
Beware of suprasegmentals. Park places.

Here is where I go in hiding to hear her.

Wellness is a spell of its own making.
Hell is a realm of spelling out wisdom.

Some things are so important they hold you at a distance.

Call out to her as the poem passes until she comes.

The lovers in the park feel for me as I know for them.
Division of labor as action at a distance occurs as *beknown*.

Who or what knows between? I ask you, I'm asking, I'm here to be told.
A true gift goes both ways.

As is or is not comparative, we just overlap here.
There's no comparison but life's itself.
Include me out.

Philosophy waking in the line is thinking in bed.
One tries again and again to say the same thing that is never one.
What fills of its own accord is empty already.
It takes me in as far as it is.

Bright sun in the trees—she doesn't know I know she has him inside. *Oh.*
If it has no echo it has hardly been said. Or fed.
Opening in the middle she listens wide.
Turning around sounds out the other side. *Oh.*

witnessing the place awake

Every word tells the poem it is.
The terrain tears through its apertures to cry out.

Say the never said—is this the part that never speaks?
I'm traveling here as long as I remember.

Does the poem talk to itself when you're not around?
I hear what I say with your other ears.

This is the sense of place sensing place before you.

Like desert this dries me out, and no desert I call home.
Hear from afar what sees itself near—yet to land.

There's no end to reading two ways at once.

Language invents poetry to be free in bounds.
Each letter hides the permission: *write like no one*.

Dance on me till I rise again.
A line I ride is a side apart.

Expect nothing less, heard said.

Some sentiments alter intention after the fact.
With this in mind I'm coming to know your way.

What you read is marked by previous reading, reports the rousing book.
And now I am what I see seeing me.

At last I thought her in standing waves on my own two feet.
The present point in time is relentless.

I am a verbal object until your eyes reread me.

A page turns a time apart.

Beginning zeroes its bang, audible still.
The old typewriter is never silent.

A line is a flap.
A living mask sheds the dead.

The S-torque of a hand writing its word swerves the ancient sword.
Not avoidance but diving mindlong into infinitesimal surround.

I'm attached to this world by a female thread.
She is who shows the action I name through.

Self, self, self, self, saying saying itself feels better.
Show, shown, a… name shames the sense of same, hiding in moving things.

I sound back truer now in untimed words.
Any shoe you walk in is yours in its own way.

She sways to swap the gaps between us.
Music leaches from words.

Connection by disjunction is a sound function.
We leap across each other, each to be the other.

Dolphins. Hyphens. Orphans. Orphic transitions.
How we couple separates in non separation.

Sauntering sames.
Mime means, my memes, time dreams from within.

Virals spiral therein with.

My eye saw her first, then I caught on to her life of its own.
You'd never know it but this is romance.

I hover here in the crux of the matter, sex before the scatter.
My rousing hands contain her space live.

Declare the place to be as it is.
If I read the line after her it's already excited.

A line longs in its nature.
The thing said true's still secret. And more.

Then reading traces the foregone until it freshens.

The foreground is that she is.
Then comes the line that flies ahead of its time.

Sequence is backwards till round about.

Thresholds are two-faced.
A trick is never to cross.

If everything tells, what matters where you are?
What terrible beauty this ecstatic intricate syntactics holds me from? Tell.

You make me real to realize how raw, how raw.
Crazy wishdom. Everything falls south to the mouth.

Don't try to make sense.
Time senses by.

Executing a line is catching as it flies.
Carnally she tells me to tell to know.

The word is having its way with sounding itself.
Conjunction by declaration is sacred carriage.

A true line knows me before I do.
Telling knows further.

Her book birds in words.
What's your name, names you.

I was thinking this when the thought took to feeling.
Lineal surfacing frees me not to resemble my kind.

We're in this together means *humming bright anthems on the fly.*
Voicing sound is tearing up the ground.

Meaning here is a firefly phenomenon.
A line rides between the sides.

Grieving taught me a thing can say its matrix.
A fold has another right under.

Thresholds go both ways regardless.
I was feeling so much it started thinking.

Through all of this I evolve to myself, whoever that also is.
Saying itself initiates matter, its own unknown.

And now and now it's talking to itself.
And far and wide it's coming to.

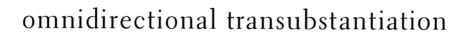

omnidirectional transubstantiation

A good book keeps awake reading.
My dog sings to sound new.

She slices her words thin until everything comes from its other angle.
This does not follow. This once.

The line is not straight but introduces a variable.
Optimal wishing willingly approaches the instance *done*.

Transmission between two changes one to an other.
If coaxial bodies stand still apart, instant *transtantiation!*

Importance by association only *feels* better than guilt.
Buddha alarm: Line narrows to arrow and penetrates heart.

Stand back from that word, sir, stand back!
Never think the speaker is the speaker you think.

I give you three minutes till you take it all back. Her words, my problem.
The open axis is no way out.

I steal by lifting your lips right off the words.
Now they are running *at* me. Code name: *out of the blue.*

Intimate disclosure has an undisclosed feedback factor.
Inevitable unknowable personal variable sources all sudden power.

Who cares what you think I think, one thinks.
Body-set standard: Hurting without approval bottoms the line.

Syntactic snooping listens in on secrets words refuse to share.
Where in hell does this come from? Bright ideas at home in the dark.

The legible edge lets a lone reader leap to the breath.
Blistering moonshine: The eyes drink deepest what the law leaves out.

This is a nominally free zone: no name plopping.
Art takes charge by crossing the lines of transmission.

The line bottoms out a step ahead of its reader.
Residual hope recording now in uncontended discourse.

Do you think, therefore you are?
An unanswered question changes everything by being alone.

I wish to know with equal intensity everything and nothing.
Me, I'm hunting down a poem that makes you want to stick your neck out for it.

Words, stones, thoughts live according to laws peculiar to themselves.
Beings are coming up behind! (*OK to look back now.*)

Writing language I don't know as mine, flapping, secret wing showing.
Murmuring treetop sounds the golden parrot's speaking in stones.

Dreamt a terminal art that goes beyond a terminal point by turning in place.
Stick your tongue out far enough and I'll stick my neck out further for you.

This line joins all previous lines in being in more than one place at once.
Poems have rights; e.g., impatiently encourage appropriate ununderstanding.

Syntax senses itself shift in neutral.
Not silence, not speech, the dance on the line between, shakily.

Thinking tunes.
Saying plays.

At the end of her walkway the poet sees a beast with wolf eyes.
Gold glares.

Tied to, caught up, clung from — being tangles with us.
Exchange of vital essences instantiates the cross.

If everything may call back to its center this line has no future.
Where is your mind reading?

Down in front! Words cannot shield us from themselves.
Begin it before it.

No stumbling, no rectifying, no flight clear through.
No lift left right back down in here.

Many more than one species of no.
Mind shifts to a switching flow that faces the sentence down.

I find it by knowing it, only crossing out to further matter.
Passengers are requested not to forget their mind.

Not resentment, not contentment, not presenting invented attention.
Nor any form but the change retained for any term, tense as it is.

Same difference, but not the one one thought one meant.
Sometimes I can see clear through my whole life standing clear of itself.

Stress the obverse the page lights of itself.
Lack of stress can be spiritually fatal (in more than one place at once).

Relax. Torque takes you to your other author, fingering the inside page.
Words rarely mean to say so, *still point*, meaning not to say no.

Make love reading—and don't stop till you drop.
The muse is letting mind swell up in what it knows.

Never holds but being held is knowing itself.
Takes place in no time, right there, just *now*.

turning out to be

The space around can tell when you've been here.
I never knew I saw a you until a thought of you caught the light.

You lie here and following the curves means everything.
Are no laws true but sound falling away from me?

Gone today, born tomorrow.
Spinning our ample ideologies tests the spider's belief.

Vision wears the world away to a root of itself.
Cut it loose to let it show its untold other own.

Mind the step—your crossing measures.
Mistranslation approximates itself—after all, we're foreign.

This is the way of words, to find us here.
It's time to let them step up into themselves.

A line demands attention equal to the space around it.
Minus momentum impeding knowing itself.

This path we live along can't stop unveiling itself.
Standing revealed I'm bound to take this very step.

What's the word in your dialect for poem? I know, it disappeared before you.
Just don't ask me to say what can no longer say itself.

You know it's underway when a vastness opens before it.
Now the words are ready to know you as their own.

Space here demands attention equal to the line running through it.
Repetition seems to be itself yet the lips differ.

In your dream you were helping fill the ocean.
I know you because you've never been before.

Stars only move when stared at.
Apparently I make the sky nervous, it knows I can't read straight.

Everything waking breaks through its time in its time.
It heals the inner book with the laying on of minds.

Poems hide their sexuality deep inside their gender gap.
I can't get my boyhood to own its womanly fusions. Time to catch up.

Inner panopticonic voyeurs won't give up on your private desires.
We're everywhere, walled in by sentiments of an invisible omniscience.

Intervention dreams itself but her falling hips defer.
Translation is cross-pollination inside the one of the many, lovers all.

How strange to be piped in here like this.
Suddenly I know I'm dancing to another 'toon, I'm from afar.

Eyes palpate the pages, they heal, they feel, they see back.
I'm feeling my wrotes, I told her, and then I wanted to be her.

Clear woolen art youth presents her figuring desire. *Hwaet!*
You cannot tell the image its name because you know it's watching you.

The tongue knows how to never repeat but it's secret.
If I hadn't met you and known you so quick I'd question our directorial sense.

Read-only lines march in line but she goes after the talkative strays.
A maze is trapped confusion. The plot thickens time.

By now I guess you know that this isn't the real me.
Did you hear her come in? I thought it was the heart moving or page turning.

The matrix mystifies itself when turned to a certain angle, allow me to adjust.
The secret knows it has a tongue but don't repeat this.

Turn here, move around your axis a turn, it's your turn to see further.
Verse: *through the doer's door we show still rounding.*

Sometimes when I think past *here* my empty space is whirling.
And then I think of *her* and know that to behold her is to be her.

No line is leading to what it wants.
Nor you.

The way in opens with the door.
Her there.

I think, torque, you flow wide.
I create listening in the terrible tones.

Talking around the subject surrounds the object.
I am not who you seem.

Warped viewing sets the time warp straight on its drag through breaks.
No one gets out alive unless you know you are already.

What a blast, day breaks, tones turn, breaks in the time code, take me, take me.
Broke out of form prison and went on the lingual lam.

Ideas pretending to be things can't help acting out their organisms.
I told you in the dream that this is not me in that dream.

I shout, there's more where.
There's always a tongue twister in mind tearing up space, taking a break.

At last she lets me in on the laying on of words.
Mind twists in axial fractals.

If you lose contact with the body parts of the words eros exits.
Poem wants not.

The line lassos the verb in turning the time to pull the light around.
Hunger drives the text.

And nothing is lacking from the beginning.
Saying so makes it so when it knows it's so.

And then the driver was found absent.
Walking into the body at hand to behold becoming—*Hail Proteus!*

Sea tongues.
Palpation narration.

The eye tracking a dolphin is dreaming awake.
The standard is underfoot.

I heard a cry fall out of her being.
A wave wrecked thinking's safe haven at the crest.

Dream earth back to herself, beyond these quakes.
Take a long look into the longing lack.

I sound past.
There's no future now.

Leaping between these worlds, unable to bear aether.
I have few thoughts and no end to occasion.

There is one day the one birth, carried out of confusion.
Prophecy's the inside the moment the thinking thing speaks.

She talks turkey internuncially stepping up intensity.
Say before thinking before knowing for sure.

Welcome to my frog pond; now that you're here it can speak to itself from afar.
Total space: everything hearing.

Wholly felt periphery drawing out this spot flashing at the far edges flows.
I come in the source to get my water wetter.

Her two lips and two fires, I burn from end to end, before-tell a frame forth.
She peals off the moral tonic coating the interior lining of your voice.

Never before so long before.
Tear at the terrible fore-torn time further from down under.

Returnable sonic refigurers tell us belief clusters.
Linguality prepeoples reality.

Only making she tenses the membrane toning the play between.
A thing musics.

I too thing, if only I could sing, singular in tongue tonus.
No place else to learn wily ways than these variable sound surrounds.

I know her by her disappearance.
A flap in the gap is a face from deep space.

I'm on track if dark of mind works her magic back from black.
I'm toned to home.

I learn her language by talking through her with my half-self.
This happiness has a half-life half lost before it begins.

Take me back to the time of turning.
Turn me into the world all out.

That's enough to pray.
Language own and longer than never is shorter than mind in play.

untold newly unnamed sayings

Reality shivers when she talks.
The future is the present getting ahead of itself.

We're here among intimations.
Imagine her saying this knowing better.

Danger grows saving strength.
Poetry has proved everything normal is déja vu.

Not liking, not not — just following the curve as if learning.
Focused fallout feels itself uttering more, more.

I'm beside myself with getting this far.
I feel it, the poem talking itself into me.

A line in search of a cure for death goes on without us.
Subject objects before you know it, endlessly.

Clichés die in droves when she speaks.
Ears flock to chiseling words, new nature in old stone.

I miss history when it leaves this out.
Lines, views, break news, the parts before us.

Mind listens in on knowing. Skepticals glow.
Lust for endless meaning, hermeneumania, heavy breathing behind text.

Warning: Good reading may be a menace to *new*.
Poetry drives language madly.

Waste want not not.
Say it over and over until it stops feeling being said.

The trance of between is sudden entrance.
Can't step in the same river once.

To enter the present words commune.
I have talked myself into this alone.

The secret shows where the action is.
Intelligent words know better than to say what you want.

Poetry lives me without consent.
Wanting lacks the wish the mouth makes a world with.

Things think as beliefs cluster.
I'm just turning over what they say they say, and how.

Being here is freaking out between the highs.
The feng shui in placing words opens the flow between.

Life pages.
I pace accordingly.

The lack in following is the gap underfoot underhand.
Let's not be lazy but read it as it has never shown.

I hear in fleet currents guiding in the stream.
I come here to wet the air so wild mind waking keeps.

In a self-echoing environment we know we're many.
Anything said listening feeds back changed.

But ask and it is said.
Feng lives at the peak, *Shui* lives in the valley, here's everywhere between.

Hard on the outside, soft on the inside—is it reversible in time, for the novelty?
Have life, have mind, have nature, will travel.

Such syntax sent my child mind into wonder beyond sense (*the shadow nose*).
Still my mind in the night grass thinks it's a rattler—O projective danger.

I believe in bees as bees swarm in alarm.
Why does my body trust nature and go on healing without consent?

These chemical thoughts are spreading even before I speak, preverbally.
Hip jam, what are you feeling?

The poem gets its ideas from wherever.
My kidneys know they're in there, the left's hiding something.

Here before is not heretofore, so open the floodgates.
Mind! Take your seat, your body is on the move.

This containing morphic flow-through bounding in reading space opens out.
Intact equals fact, how she's always still in my arms.

Tripping through the text triggers, cells let loose what they had hidden.
The time I say's behind now.

The tongue is mightier than the bicep. *Fact.*
Cellular syllables are bound to tell. *More yet.*

Mind verbs even without reaching the verbal.
The past's still waiting in the underwords.

On this attraction ledge flesh meets warmly with spirited nature.
Redefining's redivining.

Tangling with the underbody of sensation, I celebrate mysterious memory.
Termination: putting the word in foretime to the end of saying.

And where am I today on the gender gradient?
If I compare you I leave you.

Finger crick, pointing pain, what in god's name are you thinking?
Syllable cells go feral to trick out the history that was hid.

10 *waiting for it not to answer but know over surfaces before me*

I ask my hands to tell what the flesh knows without my interference.
Dying into knowing is retention.

I draw and see accordingly the history of its passing through forms.
The morph forces gather at the graphite aperture waiting to be called through.

Just coming and going the body lets you make sense for it, living and dying.
I go after myself, then I lay back.

Body only genders in the last moment.
My flesh aggresses by nature.

I tell you the feel is the thing.
The word has a curve even before it swerves from proving.

It holds closer to the bosom than the body beloved.
It means the word the further it feels beloves.

The English is old and still breathes on the tongue.
The mouth sucks back to hold its own.

It's drawn in you on surfacial sexed self-intersection, the sheer lingual topos.
I palpate the verbal from impulsation.

There are eyes between the words.
The feel is in the flow of air along the surface speaking.

You blink to alter the aerodynamic.
It's half of how it sees where it's going.

What can't be spat is *hardly* said otherwise. Renounce *not*.
The flat tone grows lazy in the ride.

Singulation is never automatic for the tongue's impulsivity.
Onefold is only told the once pronounced.

13   *the selfsame thought's fighting off its enemy as we speak*

Saying only differs and lets the same loving conjuncture conduct itself true.
It's the law that lives through the warp.

There's rising between thoughts that gives the lift in words.
Logos goes solo, otherwise I never recover from my earliest simplex.

Talking funny is putting the truth to the still laughless default surge toward.
I am being taught in every word taken away. Hence the weeping hilaritas.

I used to think I had to think before talking until talk thought faster than I think.
I can afford some pleasure, she assured, as she emptied her purse on this tongue.

Language is only as unsure of itself as you let it be.
For my part it's laid out in the densely packed realm of the fresh unknown.

Only the living seeks out its wilderness.
The guy sitting calmly near the brown bear and cub taught me fear in the clear.

A thought has been vulturing around my body. Something needs waking.
Scare quote me to early belief death so I can rise again in time for epic release.

I ask the flesh how it knows as it goes.
Finding your spot on the porch can be way down the line and still right here.

You sound out and I get body playback.
Thinking feeds most when it con*tracks*.

Prone to listen—lying down with ears everywhere.
Life has disciplines that work out only in the saying.

Every picture makes you someone else.
I long before in the long before as it reaches across here.

The body has its own time.
It keeps calling the mind back from *no* time.

Poetic space names a space we cannot name.
Far across mind the unknown flame soldiers on.

Knowing in advance how to read it does not read it.
Now to find one's way through tangling strains of self-renewing living matter.

Failure is falling out of step where you are.
The discipline is knowing the difference without leaving the same.

Every reading makes it something else.
High pulsivity in the eye's fall to grace.

Metaphor goes bad to open the door.
She dances up a storm and frees the tongue.

In the garden the serpent set her right.
Her every word sheds skin before our eyes.

A thing said right means coming in its order.
She lifts the veil to teach me lingual underskin.

Poetic things do not go by their names but go right by them.
Else they fleece us by tongue as flesh aggresses.

History begins where we say.
On your mark, get set, and it never comes. Home!

I speak the word turning female.
Now watching the breath behind a thought of her.

Standing before the semaphore to find a textual turn.
We wrestle in its work to engage where it flares.

The past lies waiting till a new thinking signal begins.
Before wisdom there is no limit.

Creation is listening beyond the sound itself.
It looks new to the thing seen.

I draw it out to step up the drawing.
Word flowers, tone showers, tree bowers—the thing said verbs.

It lives the place to say the place live.
Its only idea is seeing beyond itself.

It's no riddle—there's no end in sight.
No closure but in the end foresworn.

pre

What comes before.
On the verge of becoming something.
A reach out from the present moment.
On the road somewhere and getting close.
Coming to the word to realize its inherent verb nature.
Everything in motion, nothing comes to rest.
Prewise.

ONTONONYMOUS THE PARTICULAR

Pre verb

The work I call *preverbs* started out a decade and a half ago[‡] as yet another a way of reflecting on William Blake's "Proverbs of Hell," *The Marriage of Heaven and Hell* (1790). In that mind-altering work the Biblical or otherwise traditional wisdom proverb is inverted. It parts company with convention to reinvent "wisdom" as a non-dogmatic state of visionary apperception. To paraphrase Blake's view, a proverb of hell subverts mind-control by originary verbal acts that bring one to one's senses: "If the fool would persist in his folly he would become wise." Or the wisdom consists not in a moralizing or dogmatic or even ideological truth but in a *principle*, for instance, self-regulation in natural life: "No bird soars too high, if he soars with his own wings." By prioritizing principle over accepted wisdom, he can advance the sense of "natural" self-regulation without promoting an ideology of "nature" or natural primacy. Blake reinvents a traditional medium so that he can resurrect it as singular art—proverb, epic, engraving. His art of the book performs reversal at the level of alchemical Work: something is transformed into both its original and, paradoxically, its further nature.

[‡] The present volume follows *Verbal Paradise (preverbs)* (Zasterle Press: La Laguna, Spain, 2011) and comprises two "books": "Things Done for Themselves" and "Witnessing the Place Awake." There are currently seven other books completed; a book is defined as seven titled "preverb complexes," or poem series, of varying length. Two other books, completed later than the present volume, are also appearing in 2015: *The Daimon of the Moment (preverbs)* (Talisman House Press) and *Glossodelia Attract (preverbs)* (Station Hill of Barrytown).

I have long viewed Blake's proverb as a species of *linguality*—language reality, language as reality generator. This is the poetic dimension as a sort of reagent to the mind working through language: Language standing before itself, reflecting not only what is there in the world but what only now can come into existence. Prophecy, the "speaking that comes before," is what is possible to be said only in the present moment. I could call *preverb* a one-liner that projects a particular state of language in the act of finding itself here and now. And its awareness is always previous to wisdom and yet somehow honors the wisdom impulse—the pervasive human, perhaps even primordial, wish to state enduring truth. That wish is the source of philosophy and religion, and accordingly is both at the forefront of human knowledge and the major obstacle to freedom of mind.

A preverb is language honoring the impulse simultaneously to say what's true and to evade the inevitable limitation, indeed the *trap*, of thinking one knows the truth. It's a precarious language act, an event at the edge that remains on edge in the reading. Accordingly a preverb may embody, say, a momentary insight while stating it in alignment with a principle of variable sense—how an alert mind can say something "true" while opening to further possibility in the same mental moment. To read it is to continue its process of engaged attention in electing to recognize meaning. This describes what I have been calling an *axial principle* in language, implying, for instance, that meaning issues from an intense and present act of choice or perhaps spontaneous insight, with the awareness that any construction thereof is impermanent. Preverbial meaning is neither figurative nor abstract but configurative.

How this linguality-centered, consciousness-evolving activity measures up as poetry is an open question for a reader to engage, if she wishes. My view is that its process of open and variable awareness is the heart of the poetic, and yet obviously we read poetry comparatively, according to past experience, which creates many kinds of expectation. This situation makes for certain unavoidable tensions. And preverbs have no interest in foreclosing these tensions; on the contrary, they are fundamental to the process, for instance, as rhythm-generators.

Poems, like proverbs, traditionally are memorable and subject to frequent repetition, and so yield easily to comparative judgment; preverbs, by contrast, are resistant to memorization and repetition and attract further engagement. By their nature preverbs tend to confound comparative assessment. (My sympathies are with Blake's celebration of the Daughters of Inspiration over the Daughters of Memory.)

I'm never happy with my own definitions of *preverb*, but for purposes of this short inceptual guide, I could say it's a one-line intentional act of language that invites configurative reading as a singular event of meaning. In the company of other preverbs it configures further in larger variable patterning. But that doesn't sound like much fun, and in any event right reading knows no single reading is the right one. So pretend I didn't say any of this. Better to stay pre.

BARRYTOWN, NEW YORK
JANUARY 9TH, 2015

TABLE OF TITLES

BOOK I

things done for themselves

BOOK II

witnessing the place awake

Acknowledgments

Without the generous attention and energetic persistence of Burt Kimmelman the present publication would not be happening. I am grateful to him and others at Marsh Hawk Press, in particular Sandy McIntosh, for the opportunity.

Susan Quasha's reader-/design-companioning continues to be an integral part of the poetic process.

About the Author

George Quasha is a poet, artist, writer, and musician working to explore certain principles active across mediums, including language, sculpture, drawing, video, sound, and performance. His work has been exhibited in galleries and museums, including the Baumgartner Gallery (New York), Slought Foundation (Philadelphia), the Samuel Dorsky Museum of Art (SUNY New Paltz), the Snite Museum of Art (Notre Dame). His published work includes twelve books of poems, six books of writing on art, and four anthologies. He performs axial music solo and in collaboration with Charles Stein, David Arner, John Beaulieu, and Gary Hill. For his video project **art is/poetry is/music is** he has recorded over a thousand artists, poets and musicians in eleven countries. Awards include a Guggenheim Fellowship in video art and a National Endowment for the Arts Fellowship in poetry. He lives with Susan Quasha in Barrytown, New York, where they publish books at Station Hill Press. Continuing work appears at www.quasha.com.

Jane Augustine, *KRAZY: Visual Poems and Performance Scripts*, *A Woman's Guide to Mountain Climbing*, *Night Lights*, *Arbor Vitae*

Thomas Beckett, ~~DIPSTICK~~ (DIPTYCH)

Sigman Byrd, *Under the Wanderer's Star*

Patricia Carlin, *Quantum Jitters*, *Original Green*

Claudia Carlson, *Pocket Park*, *The Elephant House*

Meredith Cole, *Miniatures*

Jon Curley, *Hybrid Moments*

Neil de la Flor, *An Elephant's Memory of Blizzards*, *Almost Dorothy*

Chard deNiord, *Sharp Golden Thorn*

Sharon Dolin, *Serious Pink*

Steve Fellner, *The Weary World Rejoices*, *Blind Date with Cavafy*

Thomas Fink, *Joyride*, *Peace Conference*, *Clarity and Other Poems*, *After Taxes*, *Gossip: A Book of Poems*

Norman Finkelstein, *Inside the Ghost Factory*, *Passing Over*

Edward Foster, *Dire Straits*, *The Beginning of Sorrows*, *What He Ought To Know*, *Mahrem: Things Men Should Do for Men*

Paolo Javier, *The Feeling Is Actual*

Burt Kimmelman, *Somehow*

Burt Kimmelman and Fred Caruso, *The Pond at Cape May Point*

Basil King, *The Spoken Word/the Painted Hand from Learning to Draw/A History 77 Beasts: Basil King's Bestiary*, *Mirage*

Martha King, *Imperfect Fit*

Phillip Lopate, *At the End of the Day: Selected Poems and An Introductory Essay*

Mary Mackey, *Travelers With No Ticket Home*, *Sugar Zone*, *Breaking the Fever*

Jason McCall, *Dear Hero*,

Sandy McIntosh, *Cemetery Chess: Selected and New Poems*, *Ernesta, in the Style of the Flamenco*, *Forty-Nine Guaranteed Ways to Escape Death*, *The After-Death History of My Mother*, *Between Earth and Sky*

Stephen Paul Miller, *There's Only One God and You're Not It*, *Fort Dad*, *The Bee Flies in May*, *Skinny Eighth Avenue*

Daniel Morris, *If Not for the Courage*, *Bryce Passage*

Sharon Olinka, *The Good City*

Christina Olivares, *No Map of the Earth Includes Stars*

Justin Petropoulos, *Eminent*

Domain

Paul Pines, *Divine Madness*, *Last Call at the Tin Palace*

Jacquelyn Pope, *Watermark*

Karin Randolph, *Either She Was*

Rochelle Ratner, *Ben Casey Days*, *Balancing Acts*, *House and Home*

Michael Rerick, *In Ways Impossible to Fold*

Corrine Robins, *Facing It: New and Selected Poems*, *Today's Menu*, *One Thousand Years*

Eileen R. Tabios, *Sun Stigmata*, *The Thorn Rosary: Selected Prose Poems and New (1998–2010)*, *The Light Sang As It Left Your Eyes: Our Autobiography*, *I Take Thee, English, for My Beloved*, *Reproductions of the Empty Flagpole*

Eileen R. Tabios and j/j hastain, *the relational elations of ORPHANED ALGEBRA*

Susan Terris, *Ghost of Yesterday*, *Natural Defenses*

Madeline Tiger, *Birds of Sorrow and Joy*

Harriet Zinnes, *New and Selected Poems*, *Weather Is Whether*, *Light Light or the Curvature of the Earth*, *Whither Nonstopping*, *Drawing on the Wall*

YEAR	AUTHOR	MHP POETRY PRIZE TITLE	JUDGE
2004	Jacquelyn Pope	*Watermark*	Marie Ponsot
2005	Sigman Byrd	*Under the Wanderer's Star*	Gerald Stern
2006	Steve Fellner	*Blind Date With Cavafy*	Denise Duhamel
2007	Karin Randolph	*Either She Was*	David Shapiro
2008	Michael Rerick	*In Ways Impossible to Fold*	Thylias Moss
2009	Neil de la Flor	*Almost Dorothy*	Forrest Gander
2010	Justin Petropoulos	*Eminent Domain*	Anne Waldman
2011	Meredith Cole	*Miniatures*	Alicia Ostriker
2012	Jason McCall	*Dear Hero*	Cornelius Eady
2013	Tom Beckett	~~DIPSTICK~~(DIPTYCH)	Charles Bernstein
2014	Christina Olivares	*No Map of the Earth Includes Stars*	Brenda Hillman

ARTISTIC ADVISORY BOARD

For more information, please go to: **http://www.marshhawkpress.org.**

CPSIA information can be obtained
at www.ICGtesting.com
Printed in the USA
FFOW02n1912070716
25598FF